Living through grief

HAROLD BAUMAN

Lion Publishing

Lion Publishing
121 High Street, Berkhamsted, Herts

From text first published by the Mennonite
Publishing House, Scottdale, Pa 15683, USA
copyright © 1960, 1973

This illustrated edition copyright
© Lion Publishing 1978

Photographs on pages 11, 15, 22 (and cover), 26 and
31 by Phil Manning; page 3, Tony Deane;
page 6, John Stedman

ISBN 0 85648 096 7

Printed in Great Britain by
Purnell and Sons Ltd, Paulton, Bristol

When grief overtakes us,
the 'valley of the shadow' seems
very dark and almost endless.
Whatever your loss,
this little book is written
to help you to understand and bear
your grief, and to know that
it can be healed.

Sorrow comes to everyone

The crisis of grief comes to everyone sooner or later. It is no respecter of persons. It is an experience that we do not fully understand until we walk through it ourselves.

There are things which we can know ahead of time to help us when we experience grief and to help us give understanding, comfort, and encouragement to bereaved friends. Jesus showed this in the experience of Mary and Martha when they lost their brother, Lazarus.

'A man named Lazarus, who lived in Bethany, was ill. Bethany was the town where Mary and her sister Martha lived. (This Mary was the one who poured the perfume on the Lord's feet and wiped them with her hair; it was her brother Lazarus who was ill.) The sisters sent Jesus a message: "Lord, your dear friend is ill." '

Jesus came and he shared their grief in such a way as to be of help.

The breaking of emotional ties and the patterns of life through the loss of someone close to us brings a deep sense of sorrow and emptiness. These ties can be severed by death or by the sudden rending of a deep love relationship, as in the break-up of a home or a courtship.

Grief may be involved also in the loss of health, a severe financial or job loss, or in the confession of sin. The emotional experience following a significant loss, which we call grief, can come in many ways and it is right that we should try to understand it.

Stage one
Shock

What are the experiences someone goes through in suffering grief? The first reaction is shock. The death of a loved one may be abrupt, with no warning. Suddenly the news is received, 'He is gone'.

A wife whose husband was killed in an industrial accident received the news of his death. She fainted. When she came to, she wanted to know what had happened. She was told and again she fainted. This happened five times before she could stand the blow of the information.

If death follows a prolonged illness or comes as a result of old age, the shock to the family is not nearly so severe, although it is still there. The anticipation of loss moves us part way through the grief experience before the death comes; but when it comes, the loss is still real and still a shock. We may feel a tightness in the throat, an inner tenseness we cannot understand, an emptiness in the pit of the stomach, and feelings of muscular weakness.

At this stage in the grief experience, those who stand by may not know what to say. The important thing is not to *say* something. The important thing is just to be there, to share the experience. It's easy for people to give glib answers and say, 'Well, it's for the best anyway,' or, 'All things work together for good.'

The bereaved person wants to talk about the one who has died, to express grief, to accept the 'rightness' of grief feelings. He or she needs to find a good listener.

Someone caught in sudden grief may even have feelings of revolt, of not understanding, and may ask, 'Why did God let this happen to me?' This is natural in the depth of shock. There is no need, as often happens, to feel we are sinning against God by this reaction.

Stage two
Numbness

The second stage of grief is the experience of numbness, as though we are partially under anaesthesia. Things do not seem real. There is loss of feeling. We walk around in a daze, not able to think clearly. The shock itself numbs us so that we do not feel everything.

I sometimes wonder about the wisdom of giving heavy sedatives to those in grief. Often we would understand more and feel better later if we were given less medication. Heavier sedation than necessary is an injustice to the bereaved and hinders the grief process.

Someone in this second stage is not in a position to work his way through the 'Why?', even though he may ask it. This is not the time to probe for deep theological answers regarding what has happened. Rather, we can affirm that the loss is a heavy burden, a deep grief, and brings genuine suffering. Yet as day follows day, we can be sure that God our Father will provide comfort and understanding, as the presence of Jesus brought comfort and hope to that home in Bethany.

'When Jesus arrived, he found that Lazarus had been buried four days before. Bethany was less than three kilometres from Jerusalem, and many Judaeans had come to see Martha and Mary to comfort them over their brother's death.

'When Martha heard that Jesus was coming, she went out to meet him, but Mary stayed in the house. Martha said to Jesus, "If you had been here, Lord, my brother would not have died!

But I know that even now God will give you whatever you ask him for."

'"Your brother will rise to life", Jesus told her.

'"I know", she replied, "that he will rise to life on the last day."

'Jesus said to her, "I am the resurrection and the life. Whoever believes in me will live, even though he dies; and whoever lives and believes in me will never die."'

Stage three
Fantasy and reality; feelings of guilt

The third step in the grief process is a struggle between fantasy and reality. Repeatedly, in this situation, I have heard people say, 'It seems as if he is just away and he will come back.'

A boy of seven and a boy of nine were playing with their father on the living-room floor, just a month after their mother had died. In their play, as often happens, the father hurt the younger boy and he cried out, 'Mummy, Mummy, make Daddy stop.' In the silence that followed, they all realized that Mummy was not there. The boy's mind was still moving between fantasy and reality.

This experience is normal for a bereaved person, especially when the grief comes suddenly. This stage is a difficult one because of deep emotional attachment to the one who has died as a person and because of things and experiences associated with his or her memory.

Following the funeral of a young daughter, the father and mother did not touch her room. They left it as it was for a year, and then two years. Still grieving, they heard a sermon which helped them to see that the grief which comes from the death of a loved one can be accepted.

One does not have to dry-clean the clothes of the one who has died and put them in the cupboard, for fear of being disloyal to him. Rather, the things he loved can be used and shared with others. This can help resolve the struggle between fantasy and reality.

During this period there may be some guilt

feelings. The grieving person may say, 'If only we had tried a different doctor,' or, 'If only we had taken her to another hospital, then it would not have happened.' Guilt feelings like these are also a normal part of the grief process. We need not be surprised at them.

However, if real grounds for guilt feelings are present because of resentments or interpersonal injuries that preceded the death, these ought to be dealt with. Otherwise such guilt feelings may erupt in critical attitudes towards the other members of the family. But if it is only the guilt reaction of grief in the sense of feeling somehow responsible for the loss, then this can be recognized. We should come to understand that we do not need to feel guilty, as though we had betrayed the person who died.

Stage four
The release of grief

The fourth step in the experience of grief is a release, an utter flood of grief. This is not to say that grief hasn't come prior to this. Grief will be expressed in each of these stages. But when the person moves to accept the reality of the loss, then his emotions may seem to be let loose.

This also is natural. A sorrowing person should not try to repress his emotions. This does not mean that he becomes hysterical or loses control. It means that to shed tears, to show grief, is a normal and often necessary part of the healing process. It helps us accept what has happened to the loved one.

We are tempted to try to counteract these emotions by saying, 'Brace up; don't cry.' A boy whose father died was crying. Someone said, 'Now come on, sonny, be a man: men don't cry.'

This is not realistic. We do shed tears. Jesus cried. He showed his grief. The experience of releasing grief is necessary. Emotions ought not to be penned up inside or there will be an explosion and the release of this pressure may create new problems.

The release of emotions results in a cleansing, a healing of the person as the grief is shared. A young man's wife was found to have cancer. The doctor said she had six months to live. After the operation, the doctor revised the time to three months. This young man prayed that if God would spare his wife for one year, he would give his life to do anything God asked. His wife lived eleven months and he felt his prayer was answered. He went through the grief experience composed, seemingly happy in his relationship with God and the sustaining grace which he found.

Some time later he remarried, but he began to feel cold spiritually. His relationship with his second wife was fine, but something went wrong. Two years later, as he sat with his pastor, he began to pour out his heart and the feelings that were down underneath. Suddenly a whole rush of suppressed emotions broke out and he cried like a child. Only then did he find healing.

Emotions, when they come, should not be fought. They should not run rampant, but they are a legitimate expression of our feelings. In John's Gospel we read that Jesus wept with the two sisters of Lazarus.

'Martha . . . called her sister Mary privately. "The Teacher is here," she told her, "and is asking for you." When Mary heard this, she got up and hurried out to meet him. (Jesus had not yet arrived in the village, but was still in the place where Martha had met him.) The people who were in the house with Mary, comforting her, followed her when they saw her get up and hurry out. They thought that she was going to the grave to weep there.

'Mary arrived where Jesus was, and as soon

as she saw him, she fell at his feet. "Lord," she said, "if you had been here, my brother would not have died!"

'Jesus saw her weeping, and he saw how the people who were with her were weeping also; his heart was touched, and he was deeply moved. "Where have you buried him?" he asked them.

' "Come and see, Lord," they answered.

'Jesus wept. "See how much he loved him!" the people said.'

Stage five
Painful memories

The fifth step in the grief process is to work through the memories we have of the one who has died. This will take longer than the few days from the time of the death to the funeral. It may take months. We go to church and think of the vacant pew. We walk down the street and see someone who was a close friend of the loved one and pain strikes again. These memories have to be recognized and accepted.

If we talk openly about our grief from time to time over a period of weeks and express our feelings, this is healthy. This is one way to work it through. We need to find someone who will share and listen in a sympathetic and understanding way to our grief. This is grief's work.

Grief's work is slow. It takes time and involves pain to deal with these memories. We face the temptation to cherish only the best memories of the one who has died until he almost becomes an idol. If less happy memories are recalled along with more pleasant ones, together the thoughts of the person are more realistic and true to human experience.

In accepting the pain and readjustment to living without the person, memories need to be faced and dealt with. It helps to share these with people we can trust.

Stage six
Learning to live again

After we have moved through the five experiences described above, we are ready for the final phase of grief's work, the reaffirmation of life. When the loss has been accepted, the grief has been spent, and the memories no longer bring pain, then we can experience new life.

When someone dies, a part of the one left behind goes with him. There is an amputation, so to speak. Acknowledging and accepting this reality is the doorway to a reaffirmation of life. It may bring a new understanding of God's will and of his grace.

However, we ought to guard against hasty, compulsive actions. When someone dies, in the heat of the emotions we may be tempted to make a vow, saying we will do this or that. No, the decisions which God seeks are better made in prayer and reflection and, in the case of grief, after the grief work is nearly completed.

A woman lost her son when he was only seven. She vowed that she would walk up the hill to the city graveyard every day to look at his grave. She kept this up until she was an old lady. She had children and grandchildren, but each day she would give several hours to this walk.

Onlookers said, 'What devotion!' But this lady was making an idol of her son. She had not let him go. Instead of devoting her life to her living children and grandchildren who needed her desperately she was still expending her emotional energy on one who could no longer profit from her attention. Following her grief, she did not experience the rebirth to a new life.

Many people, after working through the grief process, come to reaffirm life. Their lives are invested in a new family or a new church experience. Their lives are filled with the grace of God.

These six experiences—the sudden shock, the numbness, the struggle between fantasy and reality, the release of grief, the work with memories, and finally coming out a new person—make up the grief process.

Accepting death

A number of factors condition the kind of grief experience each of us may have and the grief work which accompanies it. One of these is the expectations and practices of our community in the time of grief. In the account of Lazarus' death in chapter 11 of John's Gospel we read that many of the Jews came to Mary and Martha to console them.

In our day we have certain patterns of sharing grief, too. One custom is to go to the home, which is much better than sending a card, although a card can very well be sent. Just a handshake and whatever brief words we may share will be much more meaningful than something sent from a distance. By facing together the reality of death and the reality of the Christian faith, we can support each other in the presence of grief.

Our grief experience will be conditioned also by our attitude towards death. If we feel that death is a mistake that ought not to happen, this will tend to make our grief unreal. We need to realize that death does come; it is not a mistake. Death comes because we are part of an earthly order in which bodies get old, and die.

Furthermore, we are subject to finite decisions, we possess limitations. A person drives along the road, does not see the train, and is fatally injured. We can struggle a long time over the question, 'Was this the will of God?' Or we may choose to believe that God permits human finiteness and limitations to take their course without miraculously setting them aside.

We can face the reality of death in a helpful way. In our day the trend is to soften this reality through softening the words we use ('the departed,' 'passed away') and through funeral practices that tend to play down death. Actually to see the body before or after the funeral service often helps facilitate healing from grief.

Our view of death must include, as Jesus' did, the knowledge that the inner person does not die, but goes to his eternal reward. Although the physical body of the person we loved is now cold and we suffer loss and grief, his spirit (if he believed) is now at rest with God, which is gain and joy for him. We sorrow, but not as those who have no hope. We have the confident hope, that Jesus gave to his friends at Bethany.

A third factor that will condition the grief work is the strength of our relationship with the person who died. If we were close to him, the experience will be severe, as it was for Mary and Martha. If we were not so close, the experience will be less severe.

What to tell young children

One of the most difficult problems at the time of a death is what to tell the young children. How can they understand the death of a mother or a father, a grandparent or a loved one? Perhaps we have so much difficulty in telling them because we have trouble accepting death ourselves.

Only when we do not fear death ourselves, can we communicate trust and confidence to our children. Our children can understand that God has prepared a home for those who love him. We do not say to a little daughter, 'God needed your mother more than you did,' or she may feel bitter towards God. Rather we say, 'Your mother is with God and some day we, too, shall go to be with her.'

As one mother was telling her son about his grandfather's death, she began to cry. The boy asked, 'Mummy, why are you crying?' She replied, 'Because we loved Grandpa so much.' After a pause he responded, 'Mummy, when you go, I want to go with you.' The son had caught something of the love, the trust, and the faith that it takes to face the experience of death.

Just as children are no longer shut out of the mystery of birth, so they should not be shut out of the mystery of death. Since a child tends to think

of death as being abandoned, with resulting fears, resentments, and loneliness, he should not be further abandoned by being sent off to some distant relative. Though the attempt to protect the child may be motivated by the best intentions, it may result in distorting his emotional experience. His greatest need is the reassurance that he will be taken care of and will experience the sustaining affection of those nearest to him.

Carefully share information surrounding a death with the children at an appropriate time and place. Support them in their grief with your own love and faith.

Adjusting takes time

Another factor that affects the grief experience is how the person died. If the death is sudden, it will come as a severe shock. If it is anticipated, we may have worked part way through the grief experience before the death occurs. This is something we need to understand.

A young husband may know for months that his wife is suffering a terminal illness. Each time he takes her to the doctor he enters deeper into the grief experience. Each time they go to the hospital he leaves a part of himself behind. By the time she dies, he is already part-way through the grief experience, and perhaps a month or three months later he seems to have fully recovered and come to a new affirmation of life.

Some people may wonder, in such a case, why the husband doesn't show more grief. It seemingly did not take him long to adjust to the death. But he has been adjusting all along, having begun much earlier than the community. His interest in finding a new mother for his children, a new companion for himself, need not be interpreted as not loving his first wife. Rather, he has worked through the grief and has come out a new person ready to reaffirm life.

The manner of the death makes a great deal of difference as to how severe the grief experience will be. Even so, whenever and however the loss comes, the grief is still real.

Death is not the end

Our experience of grief will also be conditioned by how much the resources of the Christian faith are ours. The Christian knows that death is not the end, even for the body. Those who die as Christians will be raised with a new and glorious body like Jesus' resurrection body. The resource of the resurrection helps us to think of the person as we knew him. In addition, we treat the body with respect.

The Christian knows that death is not the end for the inner person. The spirit of one who has died 'in Christ' does not die, but rather goes to be with the Lord, which Paul says 'is far better.'

What is more, the resource of the presence of the living Christ is ours. As he came to be with Mary and Martha, so he will stay with each grieving believer, to help and comfort. We are not left alone.

In *Pilgrim's Progress* we read of Christian and Hopeful coming to the river of death. They notice how deep, how wide, how swift it is, and they are afraid. Suddenly, two men with shining faces and clothes stand beside them. Christian and Hopeful inquire if there is a boat or bridge they can use to cross the river. The two men reply that there is no other way to the gate than through the river. When asked how deep the water is, the strangers say, 'You shall find it deeper or shallower as you believe in the King.'

All who have faith in Jesus Christ can know the strength of his presence, helping them to deal with grief and, when the time comes, to face death itself.

The final resource is the support of fellow Christians. We stand by one another and we encourage one another. The funeral services themselves, which should not be lavish, play a real part in the experience of facing death and grief.

Sharing a meal is another expression of fellowship. One family said, 'We never imagined how much this could mean until we went through it.'

Sharing pulls people together as they stand awed by the experience of death. In the weeks and months that follow a funeral, members of the local church need to continue standing by, praying, remembering, and actively seeking out the company of the family or individual in their loss.

The privilege of loving another person deeply involves the risk of separation. We cannot have the richness of loving without the risk of parting. It is one of life's unchangeables. But in the parting we can understand something about it.

Though the parting is real and painful, we can count on the resources available to us in Jesus, to help us in the experience of 'grief's slow work'.

'Jesus said to Martha, "I am the resurrection and the life. Whoever believes in me will live, even though he dies; and whoever lives and believes in me will never die. Do you believe this?"

'Jesus went to the tomb, which was a cave with a stone placed at the entrance. "Take the stone away!" Jesus ordered . . . They took the stone away. Jesus looked up and said, "I thank you, Father, that you listen to me. I know that you always listen to me, but I say this for the sake of the people here, so that they will believe that you sent me." After he had said this, he called out in a loud voice, "Lazarus, come out!" He came out, his hands and feet wrapped in grave clothes, and with a cloth round his face. "Untie him," Jesus told them, "and let him go."'